ANGER™
INTELLIGENCE

The Workbook

Changing the Way You THINK About Anger!

Neca C. Smith, Ed.S., LPC, CAMS

Life Intelligence Publications

Atlanta, Georgia

Anger Intelligence (TM): The Workbook

For the late Lenwood & Ovedia Smith

Words cannot express the appreciation I feel for the sacrifices you made for me.
I am forever indebted.

For Lucinda C. Smith

Thank you for your love, your prayers and your encouragement.

Table of Contents

How to Use this Workbook

Congratulations on embarking on the journey of taking control of your anger and taking control of your life! This workbook can be used on your own or in an Anger Intelligence™ class, coaching or counseling session. It will introduce you to a concept in the field of anger management known as Anger Intelligence™.

This workbook is divided into 12 sections. The first section is the "Anger Intelligence™ System Analysis". Complete this section first as it will give you an picture of where you are in regards to how you think, feel and behave in anger. The next section, "What is Anger Intelligence™?", provides an overview of anger, anger management and the Anger Intelligence™ principles. The next 10 sections are comprised of the 5 Anger Intelligence™ principles in depth replete with lessons, exercises and activities.

We hope that this workbook will be the catalyst to the change in your life you so deserve! Change the way you THINK about anger!

Anger Intelligence™ System Analysis

Congratulations on deciding to take control of your anger! In order to do that, however, you must be aware of how you experience anger. On the following pages, answer each question regarding how you experience anger. We will use this information to help gauge your progress throughout this journey.

Anger Intelligence™ System Analysis

1. How often do you get angry? Place a check next to the box that applies to you.

1.		Once or twice a month or less
2.		Once a week
3		Twice or more a week
4		Once or more a day

2. How long do you stay angry? Place a check next to the box that applies to you.

1.		10 minutes or less
2.		10 to 30 minutes
3.		30 minutes to 1 hour
4.		A few hours to a half day
5.		A full day
6.		More than a full day

3. During what part of the day do you normally or often experience anger?

__ Early morning __ Late morning __ Early afternoon __ Late afternoon

__ Early evening __ Late evening __ Right before bed __ Middle of the night

__ It varies

4. When you are angry, do you normally express it immediately?

__ Yes __ No

When angry, do you normally wait to express it?

__ Yes __ No

4

5. **What physical symptoms do you have during or right after an anger experience? (Check as many as apply).**

	Muscle Tension		Sweating		Fluttering (Butterflies) in Stomach
	Rapid Heart Rate		Upset Stomach		Rapid Breathing
	Headache		Trembling		Tingling Sensations
	Indigestion		Diarrhea		Fatigue
	Nausea		Dizziness		Flushing

6. **How intense is your anger normally? Put a check mark next to the "degree" that applies.**

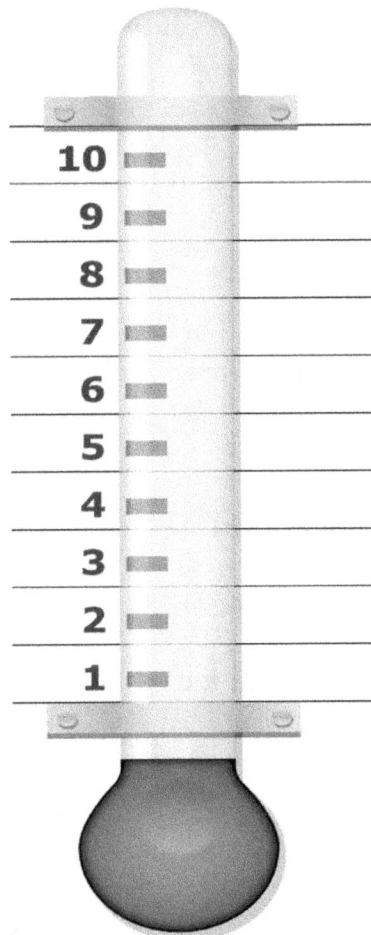

7. **When you become angry, who/what normally causes it? (Check more than one, if appropriate)**

   __ significant other or spouse   __ family member   __ myself

   __ a friend   __ someone I love   __ a coworker

   __ an acquaintance   __ someone I know well but dislike

   __ a stranger   __ an animal

   __ an object (examples: a cell phone, a computer, the TV, etc.)

   __ an institution (examples: government, businesses, school, etc.)

8. **When angry, do you normally express it to those you are angry with?**

   __ Yes   __ No

   When angry do you normally express it to someone *other than* the person that you are angry with?

   __ Yes   __ No

9. **What is normally the reason for your anger?:**

   __ Your actions (or inaction)

   __ Someone else's actions (or inaction)

   __ *Unconnected* to you or anyone else

   __ Uncertain to me, not able to figure it out

10. What is usually the purpose of your anger?

__ To express what you are upset about

__ To manipulate others into doing what you want them to do

__ To scare or frighten others

__ To escape the situation

__ Other _____

11. What other emotions besides anger do you feel regarding an anger episode? (Check all that apply or add your own)

	Fear		Hurt		Jealousy
	Disrespect		Confusion		Embarrassed
	Disappointment		Rejected		Powerless
	Criticized		Excluded		Overwhelmed
	Other:		Other:		Other:

12. When you become *angry*, check ALL of the things that you do:

_____   Hit, push, kick, fight, or shove someone

_____   Hit, break, throw or destroy something

_____   Yell, scream, or argue

_____   Name call, threaten, curse, make nasty, sarcastic comments

_____   Exercise, play a sport, take a walk or do some physical work

_____   Glare, sneer, frown, or give a stern look

_____   Roll my eyes, cross arms, use body to intimidate, etc.

_____   Control my anger and temper, and keep it from others

_____   Think over the issue and then act

_____ Compromise, negotiate, and problem solve

_____ Take a time out

_____ Be silent, hold grudges and not tell anyone

_____ Resolve the issue

_____ Drink alcohol (including beer)

_____ Take a drug (marijuana, LSD, cocaine, etc.)

_____ Eat

_____ Do nothing

_____ Other

13. How do you normally feel *after your anger has passed*? (Check more than one, if appropriate)

__ Irritated   __ Embarrassed __ Satisfied __ Relieved __ Disgusted

__ Concerned __ Confused __ Triumphant __ Tired __ Sad __ Foolish

__ Depressed __ Anxious __ No reaction or can't identify my reaction

14. What are normally the consequences of your anger? (Check all that apply)

Relationships	√	Work	√	Public/Social	√
Strained Communication		Job Loss		Frequent altercations	
Frequent Arguments		Sabotage		Legal Problems	
Strained Relationships		Strained Work Relationships		Other:	
Divorce		Decreased Productivity		Other:	
Breakups		Job Demotion		Other:	
Loss of Friends		Suspension from Job		Other:	
Other:		Other:		Other:	
Other:		Other:		Other:	

15. What are your current major stressors?(Check all that apply)

___ Financial Issues

___ Work Concerns (includes workplace conflict and unemployment issues)

___ Family Problems (issues with children, siblings, parents, etc.)

___ Relationship Problems (issues with spouse or significant other)

___ Health Concerns (illnesses, etc.)

___ Other _____

What is Anger Intelligence?

Goals: To define Anger and Anger Management
         Understand how the brain and the body process anger
         To define and identify Anger Intelligence™ and its principles

What is Anger Intelligence?

What is Anger?

Anger is defined in different ways by different people according to their experience. Some define it from a purely emotional perspective, while others may view it from a physical one. What is your perspective, how do you define anger?

What is YOUR definition of Anger?

_____

_____

According to Webster's Dictionary, anger is _a strong feeling of displeasure._

Many words in the English language have a Greek origin. Anger actually has two separate etymologies. One is the word <u>ORGE </u>(or-gay), which means indignation – that is, anger because something seems unfair. Indignation rises gradually and becomes more settled. It also suggests a more settled or abiding condition of mind, frequently with a view to correcting the situation which has caused it. You could also say it is presented as a more inward expression of anger. The other Greek origin is the word <u>THUMOS</u>. This signifies an outburst of wrath from inward indignation. This would be an outward expression of anger. Note that "Orge" is less sudden in its manifestation than "Thumos" but more lasting in its nature.

Is your anger more explosive (THUMOS) or more settled (ORGE)? Explain.

_____

_____

_____

For our purposes we will define anger as:

A NORMAL <u>EMOTION</u> CAUSED BY OUR <u>THOUGHTS</u> ABOUT A <u>SITUATION</u>.

"Anger is only a natural reaction; one of the mind's ways of reacting to things that it perceives to be wrong. While anger can sometimes lead people to do shocking things, it can also be an instinct to show people that something isn't right." Anonymous

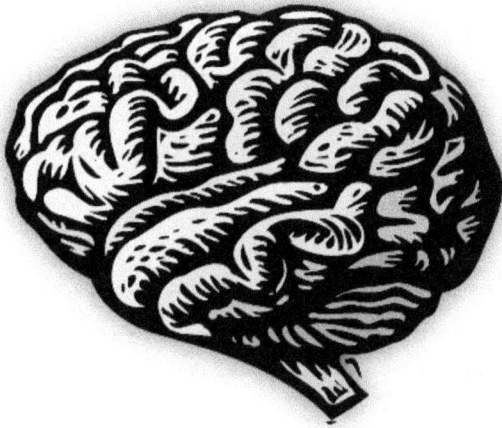

Anger and the Brain

To help us develop a better understanding of where our angry thoughts and emotions come from, we will take a look at our most precious instrument: THE BRAIN! The brain produces and regulates our anger responses according to situations. There are two processes that occur in the brain at the same time when an anger inducing situation occurs.

<u>Amygdala</u> – The amygdala is the part of the brain that REACTS. It automatically processes any threat to the individual and their environment and initiates the flight or fight response. For instance, on seeing a snake, most people will react instantly and try to get away (flight mode). On the other hand, if you see someone attacking your child, you will instantly move into fight mode. The amygdala stores unconscious memories, which is why people sometimes think they SNAP. However, this is often due to the fact that there may be some unconscious memories that they are not aware of.

<u>Prefrontal Cortex</u> - At the same time, the Prefrontal Cortex is the part of the brain that is known for its THINKING, decision making and reasoning capabilities. It suppresses the responses of the amygdala, saying, "Hey, wait a minute… what is really going on here? What coping mechanisms can I use?" If there aren't any… amygdala takes over.

The BRAIN then sends messages (neurotransmitters) to the Adrenal Glands to release the hormone adrenaline. Adrenaline causes the heart rate to increase and blood vessels and air passages to dilate (heavy breathing). Adrenaline prepares the body for action.

It's healthy to blow off steam once in a while, but chronic anger can deplete the body of energy. Anger causes stress on the heart, nervous system and respiratory system.

Health issues related to anger

High blood pressure	Heart Attack	High Cholesterol
Digestive problems	Depression	Migraine headaches

What is Anger Management?

Anger management can be defined as a system of techniques and exercises that enable individuals to recognize signs of anger and implement skills to reduce the emotions, feelings and physical sensations that anger causes.

What are some ways in which you manage your anger now?

_____

_____

_____

What is Anger Intelligence™?

Anger Intelligence™ is a term that describes the capacity to acquire and apply knowledge as it relates to anger. More simply put, it is about making smarter decisions in anger! It's more than just practicing techniques; it's based on being aware of yourself.

"Anyone can become angry - that is easy, but to be angry with the right person, and to the right degree and at the right time, and for the right purpose, and in the right way that is not within everyone's power and that is not easy." Aristotle, 384 BC - 322 BC

Principles of Anger Intelligence™

Be Decisive

This principle refers to what want your life to look like when you are in control of your anger. When you have a goal in mind, then you can decide if your approach to anger will ultimately get you the result you want.

Be Intentional

This principle focuses on being intentional about how you respond when anger inducing situations occur. When you intend on taking less destructive actions, it automatically predicts improved consequences.

Be Realistic

Being Realistic as it relates to your anger means developing realistic expectations. Developing realistic expectations about yourself, others and life in general will lead to less stress, less anger and more contentment. Our thoughts are a major area of concern in developing realistic expectations.

Be Responsible

Being Responsible, from the perspective of Anger Intelligence, means being accountable for your emotions, actions and thoughts. The idea is to always keep in mind that no-one makes you angry. You are responsible for what you think, feel and do in any given situation.

Be Prepared

Anger will come into your life, but you have control over it through clarifying and adjusting your thoughts, feelings and actions. In order to adequately respond to those adjustments, you must prepare yourself. Assertiveness Training, Effective Communication Training, Stress Management, and Conflict Management are all ways to effectively prepare deal with anger inducing situations and improve your interpersonal relations.

Anger Intelligence™ Questions to Ponder

Right Person/Situation
Is your anger or frustration displaced?
Are you frequently getting upset at the wrong person or situation?

Right Degree
How intense is your anger?
Are you "making mountains out of molehills"?
Are there some situations you have realized that you have gotten too upset?

Right Time
Are you engaging in conflicts at the right time?
Are you often tired, hungry or sleepy during conflicts?
Do you take appropriate "time-outs" before you engage in a serious conversation?

Right Purpose
Are you expectations of people realistic?
Are your expectations based on how people REALLY are or how you WANT them to be?

Right Way
How does your anger display or express itself?
How does someone else know you're upset?
Are you loud and wrathful?
Are you passive aggressive?
Is sarcasm ever a factor?

<u>Notes</u>

Be Decisive!

Being Decisive is about what you want your life to look like when you are in control of your anger.

Goals: Identify reasons for conquering anger
               Set goals for change
               Identify the 4 components of the Anger FLOW Chart
               Identify recurring anger inducing situations

Be Decisive!

It is critical to achieving long lasting change that you have an idea of not only where you are now but where you want to go. This is no different when changing how you deal with anger. Many instances of anger are a choice. However, if you have no goal in mind and see no other way of handling it, then it seems like it's not much of a choice at all. To be decisive, you must have a goal in mind, so when anger triggers arise, you will not only have a set of techniques to use but a clear understanding of what you are trying to accomplish by not getting angry. We've assessed how you currently deal with anger with the Anger Intelligence™ Analysis System, now let's where you want to go.

Here are a few questions to explore:

Why do you want to gain control of your anger?

What is the point in taking this class or using this workbook?

What do you want your life to look like 6 (six) months after completing this class/workbook?

These questions are critical to being smarter about your anger. They speak to where you want to be, not where you are. Below are some questions for you to answer regarding your goals for your thoughts, feelings and actions when it comes to anger. Think about them and then enter your answers in the boxes on the next page.

1. **In terms of your anger – how would you describe where you are now?**

    Example: "I get angry over little things."

2. **With the last answer in mind, how would you like to see yourself deal with anger differently?**

    Example: "Be able to tolerate little irritations better."

3. **If you were to make that change in how you handle your anger, what would that mean for you?**

    Example: "I could get along better with co-workers because minor irritations wouldn't bother me so much."

- Where are you now?

Present

- How would you like to handle anger differently?

Future

- What would it mean for your life if you handled anger differently?

Goal

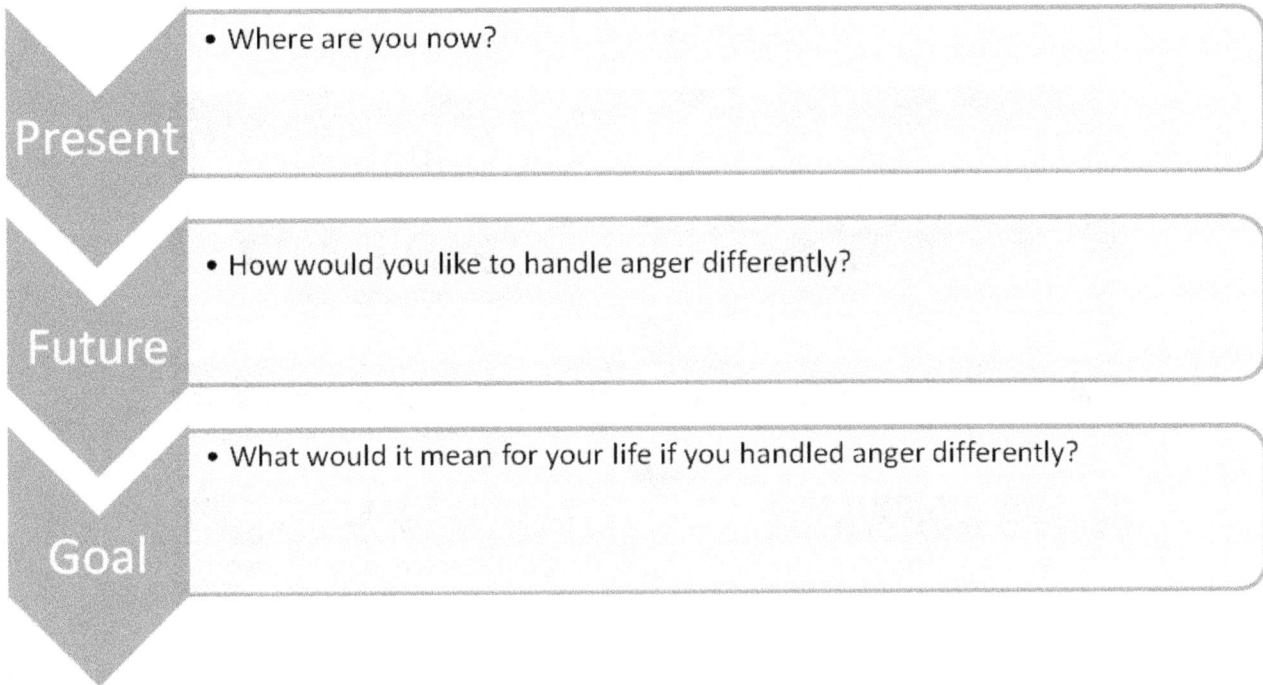

Anger Flow Chart

To get to our goal, we must first understand how anger operates in the first place. Throughout this workbook and this course we will be using what we call the "Anger FLOW Chart." This is a guide that facilitates a better understanding of how our anger begins and ends. Components of the Anger FLOW Chart are:

- **Situations**
  - o Those events or circumstances that trigger anger. Can also be what someone does or says.
- **Thoughts**
  - o These are the thoughts that automatically occur after an anger inducing situation. Sometimes called Hot Thoughts or Automatic Thoughts
- **Emotions**
  - o These are the feelings that occur after you experience a thought about a situation.
- **Actions**
  - o This is the behavior we actually engage in after we have thought about the situation. It can be what is said or done in response. These actions can be habitual.

Anger FLOW Chart

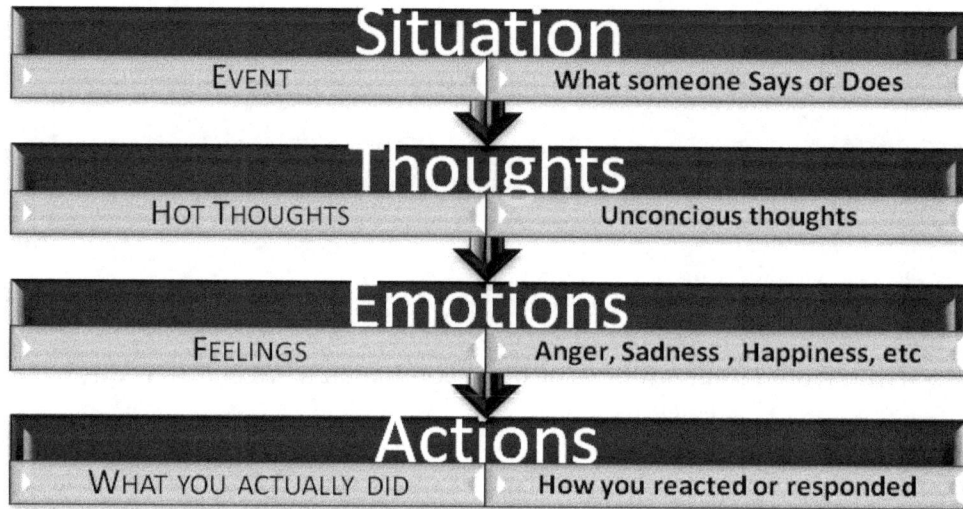

Example:

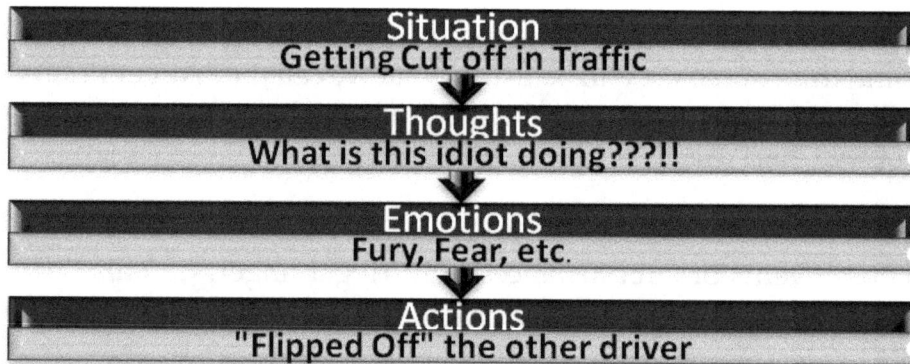

Enter 3 reoccurring anger episodes from YOUR life in the Anger FLOW Charts below:

Situation

⬇

Thoughts

⬇

Emotions

⬇

Actions

Situation

⬇

Thoughts

⬇

Emotions

⬇

Actions

Situation

⬇

Thoughts

⬇

Emotions

⬇

Actions

We will use these charts throughout the entirety of this workbook to help gauge your improvement.

Notes

Be Intentional! – Part 1

Being intentional in Anger Int1elligence™ is to about how you respond when anger inducing situations occur. When you decide what actions you want to take, it automatically predicts what the consequences will be.

Goals: Identify ways to be intentional when confronting anger
           Identify and define situational triggers
           Identify behaviors & actions used in anger

Be Intentional! Part 1

Anger is often seen as an emotion that cannot be controlled. "It just happened", some say, while others claim "I just snapped!" In such cases, people experience an event and respond with a frequently destructive, unproductive action. As we learned from our last session, regarding our Anger FLOW Chart, our anger experiences are more than just what happened and what we did in response.

Since **Situations** and **Actions** are the most apparent in this process, we will focus on them and how to be more intelligent about them. To be intentional is to intend not to get angry. It means that, in order to respond to a situation with less anger, you must first anticipate the situation and decide on productive and constructive actions. In the last lesson you identified what situations that most often cause you to become angry and how you normally respond to them. To be intentional is to be keenly aware of these components so that when they arise you don't just 'snap' or find yourself repeating the same negative behaviors over and over again. You know your Anger Intelligence™ quotient has increased when you have become aware of these and develop different intentions when approaching a particular situation.

Read the scenario below and answer the questions that follow:

Mad Shoes

"Just. Plain. Mean." This was the comment on an exit interview form by a staff member who had recently resigned from Warehouse Shoes. She was describing her boss, the store manager, Alvin. In fact, her opinion is shared by many of the 27 sales and stock room employees, who say his treatment of them is at times disrespectful and demeaning. For instance, a load of new shoes came in that were to be stocked on the east side of the stockroom instead of the west side. When they were placed incorrectly, Alvin got so upset that he yelled at his employees saying "What absolute moron doesn't understand east from west!?" They have all commented on how he "gets loud" with them when something that he doesn't like happens. Just yesterday, a sales representative accidentally undercharged a customer by $120.00. Alvin exclaimed, "How dumb do you have to be to NOT know those shoes were $250.00 and not $130.00?!" Recently, Alvin has been approached by his District Manager about the turnover in his store as well as the comments on the exit interviews. He knows his job is on the line and is beginning to see that his behavior is a problem. However, he feels justified, and does not believe there is any other way to address these situations.

What do you think of Alvin's behavior? Is it justified? Why or why not?

What could he have done differently?

Here is another view of the Anger Flow Chart that we introduced in our last session.

Anger FLOW Chart

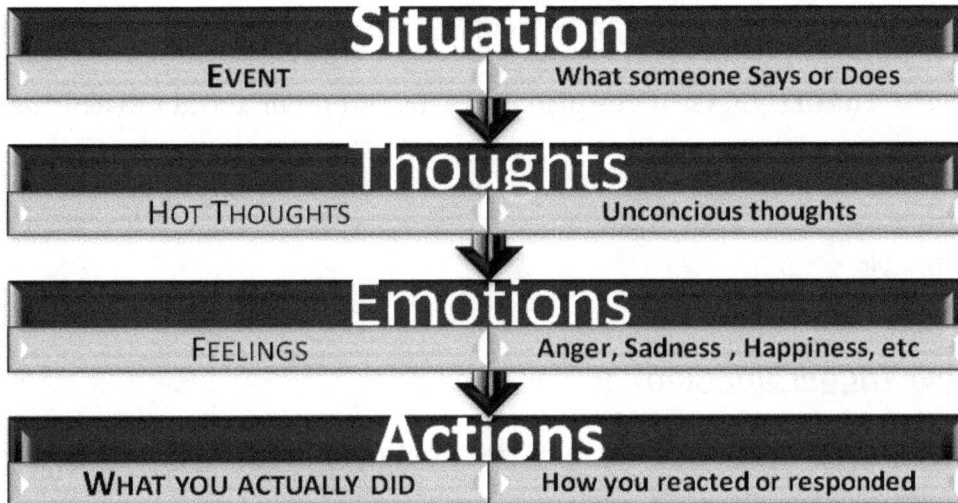

Here is what Alvin's Anger Flow Chart for **situations** and **actions** might look like.

Example:

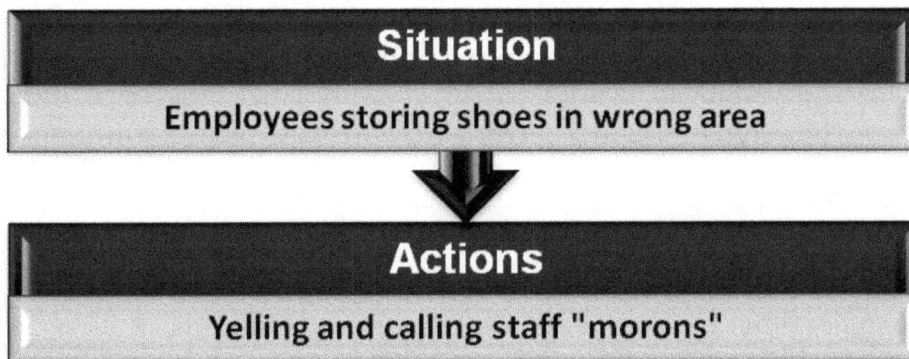

Situations

Have you ever wondered why you get angry? Our anger is normally set off by triggers. Triggers are those things that spark off our anger, and can be external or internal. Situations are considered "TRIGGERS". They can be people, circumstances, emotions, or thoughts.

Situations are **External Triggers**. Three principles to remember about most Situations are that they are:

- *Neutral*
- *Unchangeable*
- *Beyond Your Control*

Types of Anger Trigger Situations

Take a look at the chart below and circle those situations that normally trigger your anger.

Disrespectful Treatment	Demeaning criticism, arrogant or insulting attitude, intrusive behavior, ridicule, public humiliation
Unfairness	Unjust treatment, bullying, being snubbed, discrimination, manipulation, false accusations
Frustration	Hampering of ability to get a job done, blocking of goal directed behavior
Annoying Traits of Others	Finding fault in others' shortcomings: arrogance, self-centeredness, insensitivity, laziness, lying, cheating, incompetence, etc.
Irritations	Everyday situations involving mistakes, disappointments, rude incidents

Actions

Actions are those behaviors in which we actually engage after we have thought about the situation. It is usually what we do or say in response to a situation.

On the next page is a chart with different types of actions that occur after an anger inducing situation. Also included in the chart are immediate alternative actions. You can use these to reduce your reactions to certain situations. Please note they are only to be used in the short term. As you go through this course you will learn more long-term useful behaviors.

In the chart, identify which actions you use currently and what immediate actions you can take.

Types of Actions

Type	Current Action	Immediate Alternative Actions
Verbal Aggression	Yelling, screaming, arguing, threatening, making sarcastic, nasty or abusive remarks, name calling, cursing	Stop. Suck on a piece of hard candy (peppermint, lifesaver, etc). Then when you're done, say something.
Bodily Expression	Rolling eyes, crossing arms, glaring, frowning, giving a stern look, physical intimidation	Uncross your arms, relax your face, sit down, take 10 slow, deep breaths.
Physical Aggression	Fight, hit, kick, push, or shove someone; break, throw, slam, or destroy an object	Go for a walk, go to another room, exercise, take 10 slow, deep breaths.
Passive Aggression	Saying something bad or doing something secretly harmful to the person; deliberately not following rules, displacing anger toward someone or something else	Stop. Write on a piece of paper the WHO, WHAT, and WHY of your anger. This allows for some form of expression, particularly if you are not ready to express it yet.
Hold in Anger	Keep things in and boil inside; harbor grudges and not tell anyone	Write on a piece of paper the WHO, WHAT, and WHY of your anger. This allows for some form of expression, particularly if you are not ready to express it yet.
Avoidance	Escape or withdraw from the situation by distracting self by reading, watching TV, or listening to music etc. Also ignoring or denying feelings of anger	Admit to the anger by writing it down keeping it somewhere you can see it (on sticky note on the refrigerator, in wallet, etc.) and making a promise to revisit it.
Try to Resolve	Compromise, negotiate, collaborate, discuss, or come to some agreement with the person	
Substance Abuse	Drink beer or alcohol; take medications; aspirin, valium, etc.; take other drugs – marijuana, cocaine, etc.)	Go work out first

Be Intentional!

In the charts below, isolate 3 situations that frequently trigger your anger as well as the corresponding actions you most frequently take.

Situation

Actions

Situation

Actions

Situation

Actions

Now that you know the types of situations that trigger your anger and behaviors you use in response, over the next week:

1) Anticipate when the situation might occur. When might this happen within the next 7 days?

2) Decide on an immediate alternative action you will use when the situation occurs. Which immediate alternative action will you implement for the given situation?

<u>Notes</u>

Be Intentional! – Part 2

This principle focuses on being intentional about how you respond when anger inducing situations occur. Recognizing and rating the intensity of these situations and stressors will allow you to be more intentional about your actions when the anger occurs.

Goals: Identify anger intensity and anger terms
          Identify major/daily stressors
          Understand the role of stressors in anger intensity

Be Intentional! Part 2

Physical Sensations

Physical Sensations are the way your body feels when you are getting angry.

List of Physical Sensations

Place a check next to the Physical Sensation(s) that you often experience when you get angry.

	Muscle Tension		Sweating		Fluttering (Butterflies) in Stomach
	Rapid Heart Rate		Upset Stomach		Rapid Breathing
	Headache		Trembling		Tingling Sensations
	Indigestion		Diarrhea		Fatigue
	Nausea		Dizziness		

Why is it important to know how your body responds to anger?

_____

_____

_____

Anger Intensity

People who suffer from uncontrolled anger are often not aware of the intensity of the anger they feel. It is important to identify anger intensity as we continue our discussion of the Be Intentional Principle. Becoming attentive to how strong your anger actually is in particular circumstances will allow you to adjust it when it occurs.

Anger Word Quiz!

To test your knowledge about the different words used to describe anger, we created the Anger Word Quiz. Below are 10 words chosen at random that are often used to describe anger. To test your knowledge, match them with their correct meanings by choosing the correct letter.

1) _____ Bothered

2) _____ Anger

3) _____ Antagonized

4) _____ Annoyed

5) _____ Frustrated

6) _____ Outraged

7) _____ Aggravated

8) _____ Furious

9) _____ Vengeful

10) _____ Displeasure

a. To stir displeasure by persistent and petty provoking.
b. To interfere with comfort or peace of mind.
c. Destructive rage that can verge on madness. Full of extreme anger.
d. To incur dislike of or provoke the hostility of.
e. Seeking to avenge, determined to get even. An act of retaliating in order to get even.
f. A strong feeling of displeasure.
g. Implies a wearing on the nerves by persistent and petty unpleasantness.
h. The feeling of discomfort, disfavor or unhappiness.
i. Anger or resentment aroused by injury or insult by some grave offense.
j. Implies making unproductive efforts however vigorous or persistent.

Key: 1.b.,2.f.,3.d.,4.g.,5.j.,6.i.,7.a.,8.c.,9.e.,10.h

Plot the terms from the quiz on the thermometer below to identify the intensity of each word.

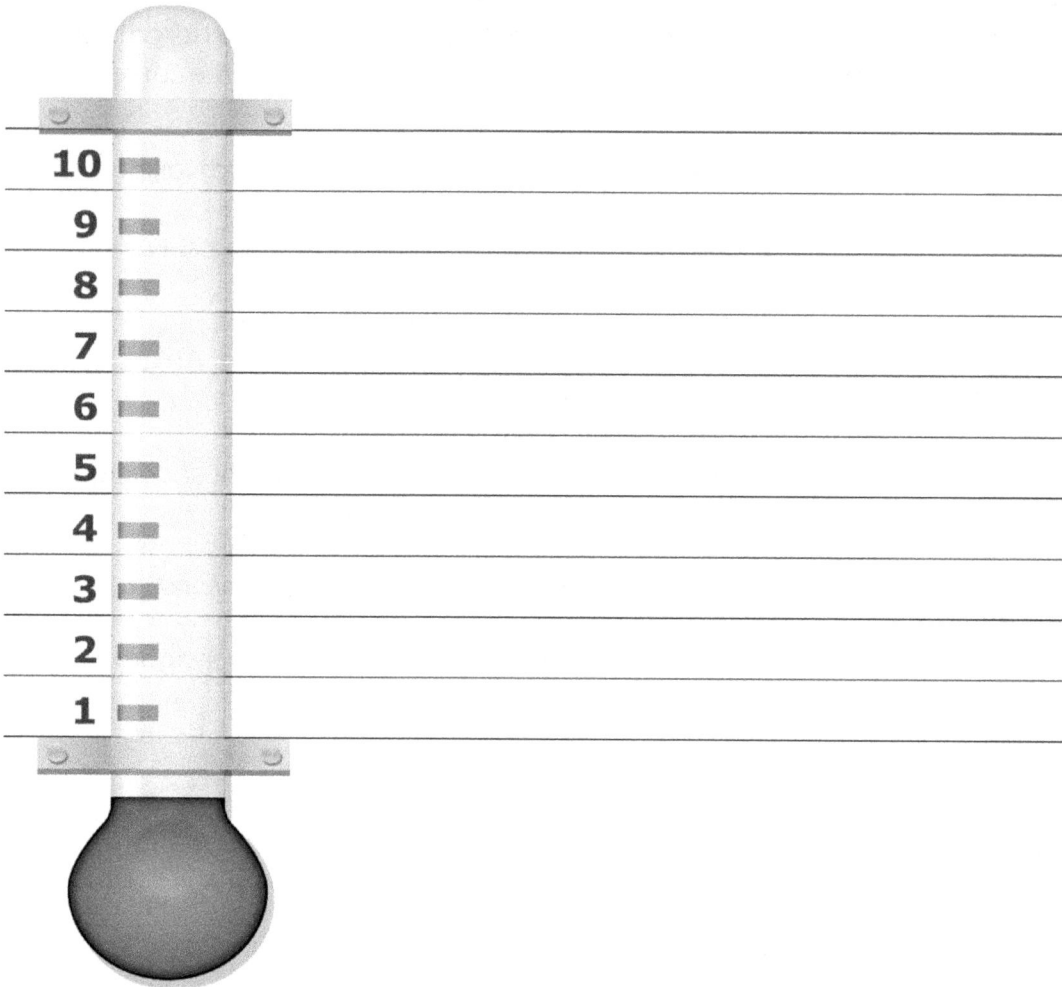

10 _____
9 _____
8 _____
7 _____
6 _____
5 _____
4 _____
3 _____
2 _____
1 _____

Current Stressors

Stressors can be a major contributor to the intensity of our anger. We don't often notice this, but when we have a pressing issue and then also encounter an anger inducing situation, our reaction or response is often intensified. The activity below will help you identify this process in your life.

From your *Anger Intelligence™ System Analysis,* look at the item 15 about your major stressors. For each one you checked, be more specific about the particular stressor, and write them in the boxes below.

Major Stressor 1:
Major Stressor 2:
Major Stressor 3:

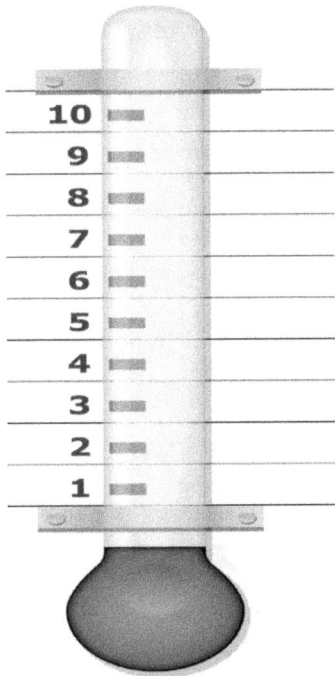

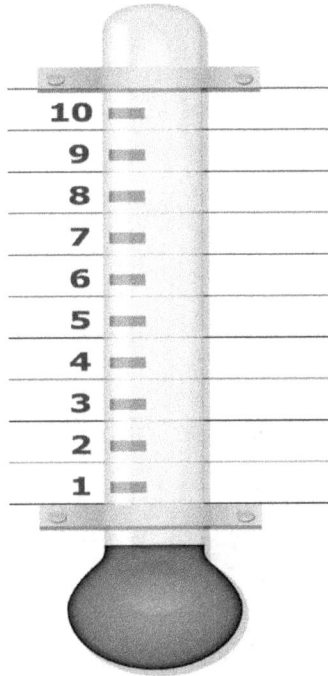

Now for each Major Stressor, rate the intensity of it. Place a check mark next to the level of intensity of that particular stressor.

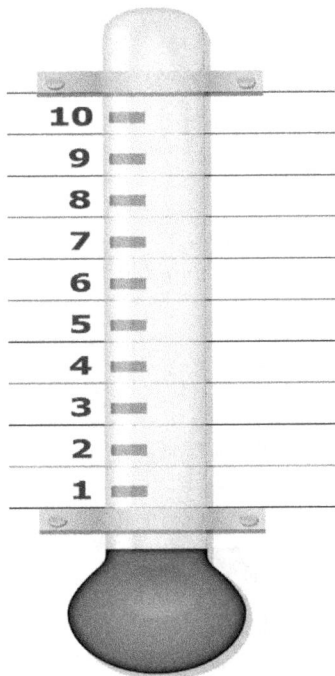

Major Stressor 1   Major Stressor 2   Major Stressor 3

Add the 3 anger inducing situations from the last lesson to the table below.

Situation 1:
Situation 2:
Situation 3:

For each situation, rate the intensity of it. Place a check mark next to the level of intensity of that situation.

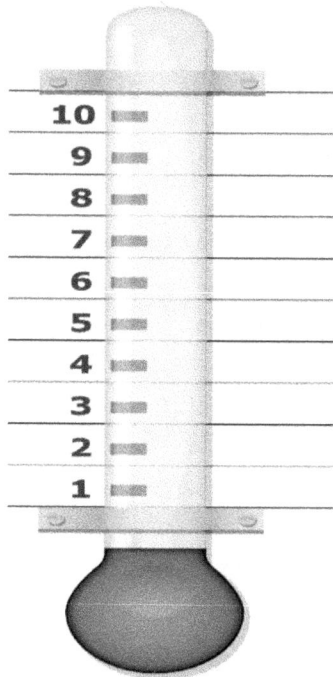

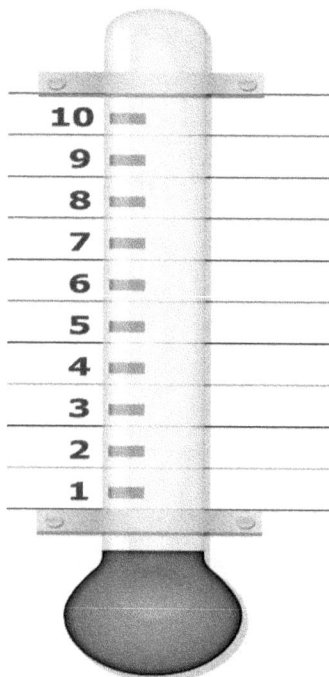

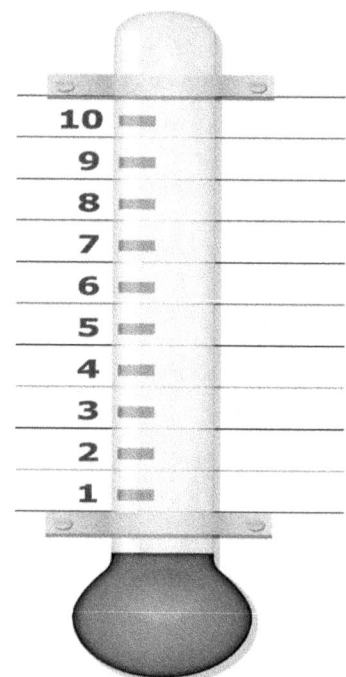

Situation 1   Situation 2   Situation 3

Next, to find out how much MORE intense your anger would be when dealing with a stressor AND engaging in an anger inducing situation, color in the thermometer by adding the additional intensity from the daily stressor.

What did you notice about the intensity of your anger with regard to your everyday stressors in combination with your anger inducing situations?

_____

_____

_____

Major Stressor Strategies

1. Complete a daily stressors list.
    a. At the beginning of the day, write down a maximum of three things that are or could become stressors.

2. Decide if you are able to avoid or eliminate the stressors.
    a. For example, if traffic is a major issue for you, maybe avoid it by going into work earlier, staying later or taking a less congested route.
    b. If you have incurred debt and are receiving calls from creditors, set up a debt reduction plan or negotiate an affordable settlement with them.

3. Reduce your exposure to the stressor.
    a. Set a specific time frame in which you intend to engage with a particular stressor (person, situation, etc).

4. Develop a strategy to make changes with regards the stressor.
    a. For example, if relationship issues are the stressors, seek assistance through counseling, reading books, retreats or workshops.
    b. If your job skills are becoming obsolete or if you want to increase your knowledge in a particular field, begin researching what you will need to do to make that happen.

We will discuss stress management later on in this course, but for now being attentive to how your stressors affect your anger reactions and responses will be of great assistance to you.

<u>Notes</u>

Be Realistic!

Being realistic when it comes to our anger means developing realistic expectations. Developing realistic expectations about yourself, others and life in general will lead to less stress, less anger and more contentment. Our thoughts and beliefs are major components in developing realistic expectations.

Goals: Define the 4 Types of Hot Thoughts
           Practice Changing Irrational Thoughts to Rational/Alternative Thoughts

Be Realistic!

What if I told you that you don't just snap?! Remember our lesson about the brain at the beginning of our course. We discussed the amygdale being the part of the brain that provides us with unconscious memories and sends us into either fight or flight mode. The most important aspect to remember is that it is those unconscious memories that cause us to believe we had an instantaneous reaction, when, in reality, nothing could be further from the truth.

Subconsciously, or without thought, you already have an opinion about how people should behave, what makes a "bad" person, what you deem as awful and what you cannot deal with it. These kinds of thoughts can be helpful in some cases in setting boundaries, but they are often unrealistic. They frequently go unchecked because we don't recognize them as being detrimental to our relationships with others. In this lesson, you will learn about these negative and how to change them into more reasonable alternative thoughts.

Hot Thoughts/Automatic Thoughts

Hot thoughts are the irrational thoughts that lead us to anger every time we think them. As you have learned, our Hot Thoughts come from our Irrational Core Beliefs. Irrational and unrealistic thoughts are those thoughts that have led to anger in the past.

> *Hot Thoughts seem "automatic" --- as if we did not even have to "think" them, as if they were already there.*

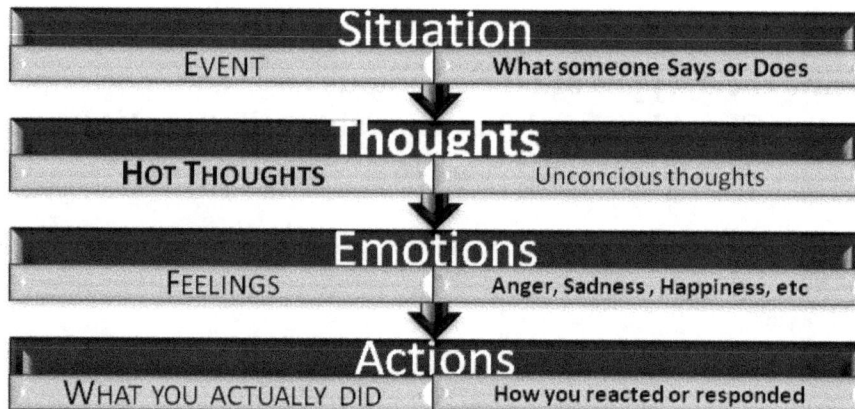

Situation	
EVENT	What someone Says or Does

Thoughts	
HOT THOUGHTS	Unconcious thoughts

Emotions	
FEELINGS	Anger, Sadness, Happiness, etc

Actions	
WHAT YOU ACTUALLY DID	How you reacted or responded

Hot Thoughts Inventory

Instructions: The following questions are intended to determine your reactions (feelings, thoughts and actions) when responding to situations around you. *When answering each question, think in terms of how OFTEN it is true for you.*

1. Do you become very upset when things don't go the way you think they should?	YES	NO	
2. Do you often say, "I can't believe it..." about the same issue over and over again?	YES	NO	
3. Do you become very upset when things are out of order?	YES	NO	
4. Do you often find yourself saying, "I can't stand it..." when you find something to be unbearable?	YES	NO	
5. Do you think people who have wronged you should be punished?	YES	NO	
6. Do you often find yourself thinking negatively about events when they don't go as planned?	YES	NO	
7. Do you find yourself often judging people because of their actions?	YES	NO	
8. Do you often get upset when you have to wait in long lines, sit in traffic, etc?	YES	NO	
9. Do people ever tell you that you make a "mountain out of a molehill," or a big deal out of nothing?	YES	NO	
10. Do you often put yourself down when you make a mistake?	YES	NO	
11. Do you think those close to you should know how you feel without you telling them?	YES	NO	
12. Do you often exaggerate how "awful" or "terrible" something is?	YES	NO	
13. Are you often impatient when things are not done in your own time frame?	YES	NO	
14. Do you feel the only way to do something is your way?	YES	NO	
15. Are you better than people whose values differ from yours?	YES	NO	
16. Are the words "always" and "never" often ways you describe the negative actions of people?	YES	NO	

Scoring Instructions:
For each "YES" give yourself 1 point then add them up for your total:

D: 1: _____   3. _____   11. _____   14. _____   = TOTAL D   _____

C: 5. _____   7. _____   10. _____   15. _____   = TOTAL C   _____

A: 6. _____   9. _____   12. _____   16. _____   = TOTAL A   _____

L: 2. _____   4. _____   8. _____   13. _____   = TOTAL L   _____

Be Realistic!

Hot Thought	Demandingness	Awfulizing	Condemning	Low Frustration Tolerance (LFT)
Definition	The idea that everything should and must go a certain way. Look for words like **should, must, need to, ought**, etc. Unreasonable expectations that we hold of ourselves, others, and the world in general.	Thinking in extreme negative terms. (Making mountains out of molehills.) Look for words like **terrible, horrible and awful**. Words like **always** and **never** are cues as well. They are gross exaggerations about reality.	The thought of putting yourself or others down. Beliefs that stem from the idea that people who don't meet my expectations or some moral obligation deserve to be punished.	Thought that comes from the expectations that things must go smoothly for us or we will not be able to stand it.
Common Thoughts	*"I shouldn't have to deal with these headaches!"* *"Traffic shouldn't be so heavy at this hour."* *"It should not be that hard!"*	*"I can't believe they're gossiping again!"* *"It's terrible that I got passed over for that promotion."*	*"He flew off the handle again, he's hopeless."* *"Every time I try, I fail."* *"My coworker is stupid!"*	*"I cannot stand it when I have to wait in line."* *"I'm going to snap if I don't get a raise this year!"*
Response to Hot Thought	Identify what are needs and what are wants. Realize your preferences Learn to accept others and situations as they are, **NOT** as you would like them to be.	Learn to think in moderate terms Avoid extreme thinking (either positive or negative)	Rate the behavior not the person. Learn to accept others and yourself.	Accept the reality of frustration and keep its "badness" in perspective Expect to experience appropriate negative emotions like annoyance and disappointment. But avoid exaggerating these emotions by telling yourself you can't stand them.
Alternative Thought	*"This job comes with its share of problems at times."* *"It's 4pm, so I expect a good amount of traffic."* *"This is not easy."*	*"It's easy to believe their gossiping again."* *"I didn't get this promotion but I will try again or look for another job outside of the company."*	*"He gets really upset a lot."* *"Sometimes I fail, but I'll keep trying."* *"Sometimes my co-worker bothers me by what she says."*	*"I don't like waiting in line."* *"I will be upset if I don't get a raise this year."*

Decide whether the Hot Thought is Demanding, Condemning, Awfulizing or LFT (Low Frustration Tolerance) and write this in box with the Hot Thought. Then, come up with an appropriate Alternative Thought for the situation.

Hot Thought	Alternative Thought
He never does his job! (Awfulizing)	Sometimes he does his job.
That idiot cut me off!	
Life should be easier.	
I can't believe their gossiping again.	
Things never work out.	
They shouldn't say those things.	
You need to be here on time.	
I can't stand it when this happens.	
They never treat me the same way they treat her and that's not fair.	
Things always go wrong.	
You should know how I feel.	
What a jerk!	
It's Saturday night, you'd think they would have a table for us!	
I can't take this traffic!	

Be Realistic!

Learning to recognize and change Hot Thoughts to Alternative Thoughts may seem like a daunting task. However, if you just choose one thought that you use that is not benefiting you and begin to think of alternatives, you will be well on your way to Anger Intelligence™!

Notes

Be Responsible! – Part 1

Being Responsible, from the Anger Intelligence™ perspective, means being accountable for your emotions, actions and thoughts. The idea is to always keep in mind that no one makes you angry. You are responsible for what you think, feel and do in any given situation.

Goals: Identify primary emotions related to anger

Be Responsible!

Emotional Triggers

The word *emotion* is derived from the Greek word "Motivas" (which is related to the word motivation) which means "*to move around or to agitate*". Thus, an EMOTION is *action resulting from situations that enhance or threaten a goal.* For example, to the degree to which I'm emotional, I perceive a threat to my goal (negative emotion) or significant progress toward my goal (positive emotion). Thus, our anger and any other negative emotion is a result of our goals being either threatened or thwarted.

Emotional Triggers are the primary emotion that has led to your anger.

How we REALLY feel about a situation can be deeply hidden, yet when it surfaces, it does so as anger.

Pursuing a Goal:

What did you want to happen in the situation?

Threat to Goal:

What stopped the situation from happening?

Emotion Word Matrix

This Emotion Word Matrix gives you only a sampling of emotional triggers and their intensity. However, it will be helpful on your journey to identifying your primary emotion.

Category	HIGH	MODERATE	LOW
Happy	Excited Overjoyed Ecstatic	Cheerful Lively Elevated	Pleased Glad Content
Sad	Depressed Hopeless Despair	Discouraged Miserable Upset	Unhappy Down Disappointed
Scared	Frightened Terrified Paralyzed	Troubled Afraid Fearful	Anxious Timid Worried
Angry	Belligerent Enraged Furious	Annoyed Aggravated Grouchy	Displeased Irked Unpleasant
Confused	Speechless Chaotic Baffled	Disturbed Perplexed Lost	Unsure Indecisive Uneasy

Complete the exercises below and use the Emotion Word Matrix to answer the questions:

The angry parent of a 16 year old has to attend a parent-teacher conference because their child has not completed or turned in any homework assignments all year. This parent works long hours to provide for the household and is not always able to check up on their child and their homework. What primary emotion might this parent be feeling besides anger?

_____

Why might the parent be feeling this way?

_____

_____

Be Responsible!

A frustrated manager is having his third meeting with a staff member who has not performed up to the standards of their job. The manager has only been in his position for six months and is very aware that he does not communicate well. The manager has also been reprimanded because of the performance of his team. What primary emotion might this person be feeling?

_____

Why might the manager be feeling this way?

_____

_____

A woman is furious when she finds out that her fiancé has to go out of town for an unplanned business trip. It has been over 6 months since they have had any quality time together and in addition to that they rarely talk on the phone or communicate any other way. What might this person be feeling?

_____

Why might the woman be feeling this way?

_____

_____

Anger FLOW Chart

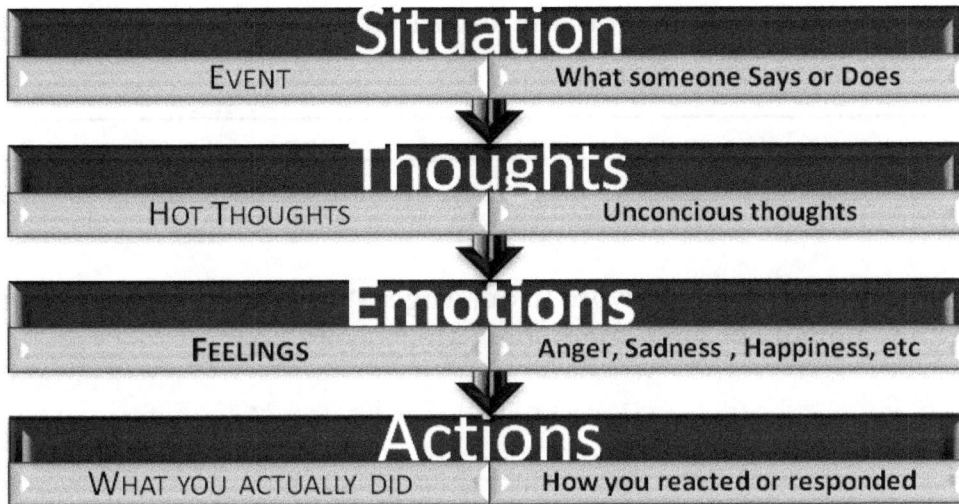

Situation	
EVENT	What someone Says or Does

Thoughts	
HOT THOUGHTS	Unconcious thoughts

Emotions	
FEELINGS	Anger, Sadness , Happiness, etc

Actions	
WHAT YOU ACTUALLY DID	How you reacted or responded

Enter an Anger Episode in the Anger Flow Chart below:

Situation

Thoughts

Emotions

Actions

Be Responsible!

Using the situation listed in your Anger Flow Chart answer the following questions:

1. **What did you want to happen in the situation?**

   _____
   _____
   _____

2. **Using the appropriate anger word (from Anger Word Intensity exercise on page 32) to define the intensity of your anger, how angry were you?**

   _____

   a. **Why were you (bothered, annoyed, enraged, etc)?**

      _____
      _____
      _____

   b. **Using the emotion word matrix, describe how the answer in *item a* (above) made you feel. This is your primary emotion.**

      _____

Our primary emotions not only cue us in to why we are angry but also the reason it is so intense in certain situations. When you feel yourself (physical sensations) beginning to get angry, learn how to access emotional triggers by asking yourself, " I feel myself getting angrier, but what else am I feeling?"

<u>Notes</u>

Be Responsible! – Part 2

Being Responsible from the perspective of Anger Intelligence™ means being accountable for your emotions, actions and thoughts. Much of what we are angry about is beneath the surface, in our unconscious beliefs. Since our beliefs unconsciously drive how we think, feel and act, it would be prudent to uncover them (as much as we can) in order to handle our anger more intelligently.

Goal: Identify unconscious irrational beliefs associated with hot thoughts

Be Responsible! Part 2

Beliefs

Much of how we act, think and feel is dependent on our beliefs. What we see and feel on the surface is only just the beginning of what we unconsciously believe. Our beliefs are those things that we accept as true. They operate much of the time in an unconscious manner and serve to help us understand why it is we feel, act and think a certain way.

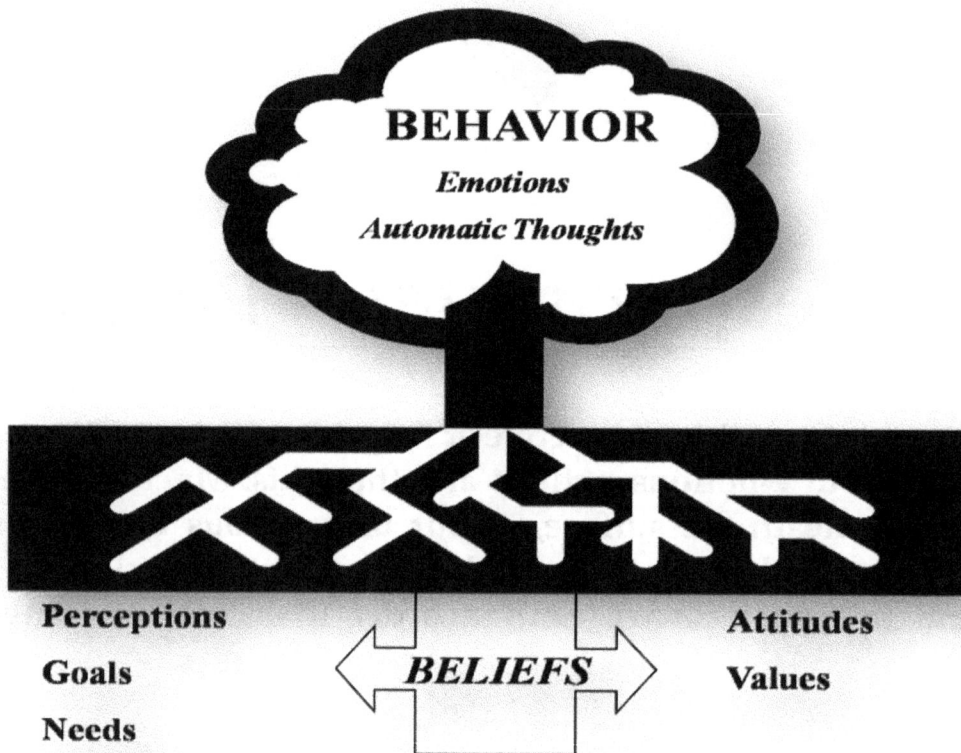

Our Beliefs are impacted by our perceptions, goals, needs, attitudes and values.

Components of Beliefs

Beliefs: Those things we accept as true.	
Perceptions: The way we see things.	Goals: What we want to happen - our desired outcomes.
Values: What we find most important.	Needs: The minimum requirements of life and health.
Attitude: An opinion or disposition about something.	

Here is an example of how unconscious irrational beliefs affect our lives:

Maria is a busy direct sales representative. Whenever she makes a request and it is does not receive a prompt response from others she immediately dismisses and labels them as "unreliable". On the surface, it looks though she doesn't give people a chance to prove themselves. Upon further examination, however, it becomes apparent that her hot thought is that she doesn't have time for "slow & undependable" people. In conclusion, her core belief might be that people only care about themselves and care nothing about her (her time, energy, etc).

Irrational Beliefs

Irrational beliefs are unhealthy, ineffectual underlying rules that guide how people react to the events and circumstances in their lives.

Which core beliefs are guiding your thoughts?

Take a moment and contemplate each phrase. Allow your mind to quickly react to each one and take note of what comes to you. Move on to the next phrase only when you feel ready to do so.

I am...
I am not...
Women are...
Men are...
People in general are...
I am not good with...
I will never be able to...
I don't deserve...
My family...
I always...
I never...
I should...
I have to...
I can't stand...

Next, go through your list and circle the phrases that may contribute to your anger.

Step 1: *Identify the belief.* From one of the phrases you circled on the previous page, identify a belief that may be a contributor to your anger from the list below.

I feel like a victim	I can't handle rejection
Something is wrong with me	I can't handle failure
Something is wrong with others	I'm afraid of success
Something is wrong with the world	I'm afraid of pain
I am not good enough to have what I want	I can't have what I want
I don't deserve the best in life	Life is a struggle
I'm afraid of being controlled	Nobody cares about me
I'm unlovable	I am unwanted

Step 2: *How does this belief make me feel?* From the Emotion Word Matrix on page 47, identify two to three feelings this belief elicits in you.

_____

_____

_____

Step 3: *Where did this belief come from?* Did it come from your parents, peers, spouse, culture, religion, society, etc?

_____

_____

Step 4: *Is this belief completely true?* Was it true in a time past and no longer true now? Have you had an experience where it was not true at all?

_____

_____

Step 5: *If the irrational belief is not true, what would be a more honest belief?*

_____

_____

_____

Step 6: ***What action(s) can I take that will reflect my new beliefs?*** *Having identified your new beliefs, it is important to put them into action. Soon you will form new habits and see a dramatic improvement in your emotions, thoughts and actions.*

_____

_____

_____

<u>Notes</u>

Be Prepared! – Assertiveness

Over the last few lessons you've learned that, while anger is inevitable, you have control over it through clarifying and adjusting your thoughts, feelings and actions. In order to adequately respond to those adjustments, you must prepare yourself. Assertiveness is a way of preparing that emphasizes communicating with others in a manner that is not only respectful but honest.

Goals: Identify different styles of communication
          Practice assertive communication techniques

Be Prepared! Assertiveness

Before we get started in this lesson, let's figure out what your communication style is by answering the questions below. Answer *Yes* or *No* to each question.

1. Do you say something when you think someone is being unfair?
2. Do you respond considerately when there is a difference of opinion?
3. Are you able to openly express love, care and concern?
4. Do you persist in arguing with someone after they have had enough?
5. Are you hesitant to share your thoughts and feelings during a discussion or debate?
6. Are you able to say no when someone is forcing you to buy or to do something?
7. When angry do you yell, name call or put others down?
8. If you are displeased with a meal at a restaurant, do you speak with the waitress about correcting the situation?
9. Do you avoid certain people or events for fear of embarrassment or humiliation?
10. Do you criticize the ideas, opinions and actions of others?

Now that you've answered each question, we will identify the types of communication that corresponds with your answer.

Styles of Communication

Aggressive Communication

A form of communication that focuses on being in control. Aggressive communicators stand up for their rights but do so by violating the rights of others. Words used to describe aggressive communicators are: arrogant, bully, bossy, domineering, and overbearing. (YES: 4, 7, 10)

Passive Communication

A form of communication that is defined by avoiding conflict and pleasing others. Passive communicators tend to hold in their true feelings and don't stand up for their own rights. Words used to describe passive communicators are: timid, scared, submissive, apologetic, and indecisive. (YES: 1, 5, 9)

Passive-Aggressive Communication

A form of communication that is defined by indirectly expressing negative or angry feelings. Passive-Aggressive communicators express themselves by appearing cooperative on the surface but show their true feelings by using criticism, procrastination, or even sabotage among other tactics. Words used to describe passive-aggressive communicators are: sarcastic, manipulative, resentful, and undermining.

Assertive Communication

A form of communication that focuses on understanding others and being understood by others. Assertive communicators stand up for their rights without violating the rights of others. Words used to describe assertive communicators are: rational, understanding, honest, fair and responsible. (YES: 2, 3, 6, 8)

Using the continuum below, place a mark where you think your communication style may lie.

Passive   **Assertive**   **Aggressive**

Why do you describe your communication style in this way?

_____

Assertive Communication Techniques

Now we will take a look at six different techniques that you can put to use immediately.

Assertive Communication Techniques

1. "I" Statements
2. Broken Record
3. Fogging
4. Negative Assertion
5. Negative Inquiry
6. Time Outs

1. "I" Statements

"I" statements are the cornerstone of Assertive Communication because they allow individuals to express their feelings, wants, and needs without blaming others. They also allow individuals to process and express their primary emotions and become responsible for their feelings.

"I" Statements are formulated in this way:

I feel _**emotion**_ because/when _**reason**_ . I would like _**desired outcome.**_

Example: *I feel disrespected when you come home late. I would like for you to come home at a reasonable time.*

Construct an "I" Statement using a situation from your life:

1) What is my PRIMARY emotion (besides anger)? (*Think back to the Emotion Word Matrix*)

   I feel _____

2) Why do I feel this way? What is the reason I feel this emotion?

   When/Because _____

3) What reasonable outcome would I like?

   I would like _____

Now try this with two more situations:

   I feel _____

   When/Because _____

   I would like _____

   I feel _____

   When/Because _____

   I would like _____

Remember that even though you are expressing a need or want – your goal is to be UNDERSTOOD, EVEN if the other person does not respond to your request in the way you would like them to!

Convert these **YOU** statements into **I** Statements

"YOU" Statements	"I" Statements
You make me sooo mad!	*I am so mad!*
You're getting on my nerves	*I am very tense and anxious right now*
You never listen to me.	*I want you to listen to me.*
You are so lazy!	
You never do anything right!	
You are such a butthole!	
You don't care about me.	

2. Broken Record

The Broken Record is an effective technique when setting boundaries if someone is not respecting what you have to say. This is best used in commercial situations rather than with those with whom you have any kind of personal relationship. It is helpful in avoiding manipulation and arguments. Repeat your statement calmly and exit if need be.

Helpful "Broken Record" Statements:

"No thank you."

"Not today."

"I'm sorry you feel that way."

"We have a different opinion."

"I understand but I'm not interested."

3. Fogging

The fogging technique is used when being criticized by focusing on the important facts but ignoring harsh, critical statements by others. Use words like might, maybe, or sometimes.

Example:

You're irrational!

Fogging Response: "Sometimes my thinking isn't rational."

4. Negative Assertion

Accepting the truth of a criticism and stating it in positive terms.

Example:

You're irrational!

Negative Assertion: *"You're right, sometimes I don't think as clearly as I could."*

5. Negative Inquiry

When responding to negative criticism, asking for constructive criticism.

Example:

You're irrational!

Negative Inquiry Response: *"Can you tell me what I said that was irrational?"*

6. Time-Out

Time-Outs are used most effectively when an argument or conversation is getting out of control. It is a technique used to diffuse anger and diminish conflict. It is different from just walking out because it involves setting rules and guidelines with others.

Rules for Time Out

1. Make a time out contract. Talk to your partner and agree to use time-outs as a way to manage conflict.
2. Decide on a signal or phrase you will use to signal the need for a time-out. Example: *I need to take a timeout; I can't express myself right now.*
3. Leave immediately or just stop talking if you cannot leave the other person's presence.
4. Set a time limit beforehand. Give yourself at least an hour but not over 2 hours.
5. Come back at the designated time.
6. No drinking or drugs during the time-out.
7. During that time, take a walk or exercise. Also, think about what it is you want to say. Use an "I" statement if appropriate.

Assertive communication is the key to gaining respect. Always keep in mind that you have a choice between being assertive, aggressive or passive. Choose the one that will have a more rewarding and fulfilling impact on you and those you engage with most.

What Assertive Communication Technique will you practice this week?

_____

Notes

Be Prepared! –
Effective Communication

Effective Interpersonal Communication Training is another important concept to prepare yourself to express your point of view articulately but to also listen to and understand others.

Goals: Identify the interpersonal communication process
Identify verbal and non-verbal communication barriers
Practice active listening skills

Be Prepared! Effective Communication

How important is communication to you? How skillful are you at articulating your own wants and needs? Does your body language, tone of voice, or gestures say more than your words say? When you communicate in anger, how well do you think your message gets across?

Effective and productive interpersonal communication is essential to the quality of our intimate, family and work relationships. Let's begin our discussion of communication by looking at the interpersonal communication process.

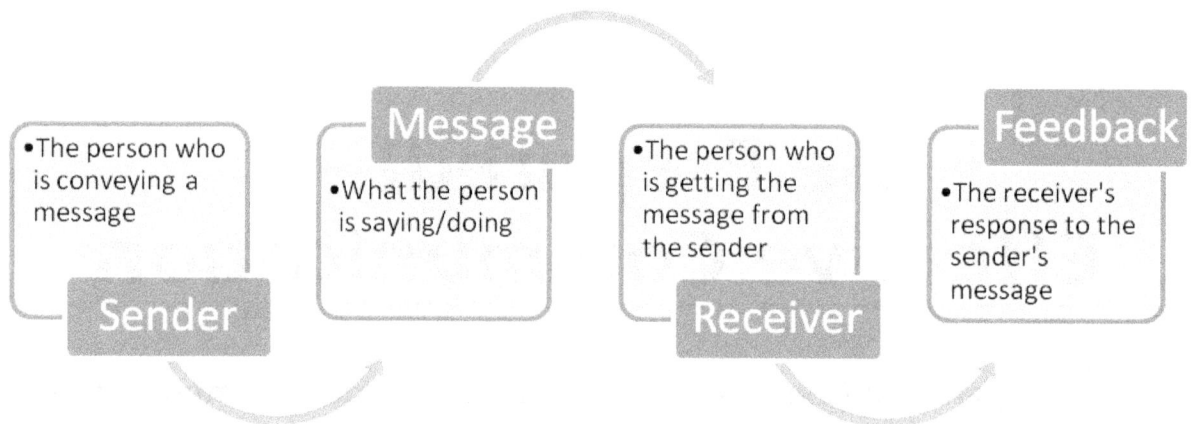

Interpersonal Communication Process

Sender
•The person who is conveying a message

Message
•What the person is saying/doing

Receiver
•The person who is getting the message from the sender

Feedback
•The receiver's response to the sender's message

Communication is successful ONLY when the message received is the SAME message that has been sent.

An example of an Angry Interpersonal Communication Process

When you're angry, do you communicate in above manner? It is impossible to have a productive conversation in an argument. Thus, it is critical that, in becoming interpersonally effective, we must learn useful and productive communication skills.

Verbal Communication

People tend to communicate verbally in different ways: Aggressively, Passively, Passive-Aggressively and Assertively. As stated in the previous lesson, Assertive Communication is the most desired form of communication for successfully getting your message across.

Angry Verbal Communication	Productive Verbal Communication
Yelling, Screaming	Calmly talking out the issue
Interrupting the speaker	Listening to the speaker before you respond
Finishing the speakers sentences	Waiting for the speaker to finish
Not asking questions	Asking questions to clarify and understand the speaker
Asking questions without waiting for a response	Listening for the answers in order to obtain a response
Tuning out	Listening

Which of these forms of communication do you use most often?

Non-Verbal Communication (What are you saying WITHOUT saying it?)

Much of what we express is through our non-verbal communication, or the things that we don't say that say so much. It has been reported that non-verbal communication accounts for 90% of our communication. What you actually say can be totally overshadowed by your non-verbal communication.

Non-Verbal Ways of Communicating

- Facial Expressions
- Tone of Voice
- Gestures
- Use of Touch

Angry Non-Verbal Communication	Productive Non-Verbal Communication
Rolling eyes or glaring	Direct yet appropriate eye contact
Smirking, Scowling, Grimacing	Smiling or neutral facial expression
Pounding on a table, kicking objects, throwing things, folding arms, hands on hips	Nodding or physically turning toward the speaker
Yelling or screaming	Speaking in a calm, audible tone of voice
Pushing, shoving, hitting, blocking the path of the speaker	Keeping an appropriate distance from the speaker

Look back at the two preceding charts regarding Angry Verbal and Non-Verbal Communication. Which of these do you use on a regular basis?

_____

_____

_____

How has it affected your intimate relationships?

_____

_____

Your relationships with family members?

_____

_____

Your relationships with friends?

_____

_____

Your work relationships?

_____

_____

What part of your communication would you like to change and why?

_____

_____

Why do you think it has been so difficult for you to change your way of communicating?

_____

_____

Listen Like a Therapist! (Or Active Listening)

Listening is just as, if not more, important than speaking in the interpersonal communication process. In anger, we often turn off our "ears" and refuse to listen to the speaker, especially if the speaker is saying something that has triggered the listener's emotions. Therapists, counselors and most people who work in the mental health field are trained to listen actively and to respond with clarity. How well do you listen? Let's assess it with the following inventory:

Active Listening Inventory

1. I want to listen to what others have to say when they are talking.

□Almost always □Often □Sometimes □Seldom □Almost Never

2. I am good at summarizing what others have said.

□Almost always □Often □Sometimes □Seldom □Almost Never

3. By listening, I can guess a speaker's intent or purpose without being told.

□Almost always □Often □Sometimes □Seldom □Almost Never

4. I nod appreciatively at intervals when people are speaking.

□Almost always □Often □Sometimes □Seldom □Almost Never

5. I keep control of my opinion when listening to others speak so that it won't affect my understanding of the message.

□Almost always □Often □Sometimes □Seldom □Almost Never

6. I analyze my listening errors so as not to make them again.

□Almost always □Often □Sometimes □Seldom □Almost Never

7. I listen to the complete message before coming to a conclusion about what the speaker has said.

□Almost always □Often □Sometimes □Seldom □Almost Never

8. I don't engage in other activities (e.g., watching TV) while others are trying to tell me something.

□Almost always □Often □Sometimes □Seldom □Almost Never

9. I ask questions when I don't fully understand a speaker's message.

□Almost always □Often □Sometimes □Seldom □Almost Never

10. I am aware of whether or not a speaker's meaning of words and concepts is the same as mine.

□Almost always □Often □Sometimes □Seldom □Almost Never

How to score:
Almost always = 5
Often = 4
Sometimes = 3
 Seldom = 2
Almost Never = 1

Disengaged (0 - 27)

The disengaged listener detaches from the interpersonal communication process and becomes the object of the sender's message rather than its receiver. This listener is extremely inattentive, and usually impatient, uninterested, or easily distracted. This person will not attempt to engage with the listener much or at all, as evidenced by slumped or inattentive posture and no direct eye contact.

Inactive (28 - 37)

The inactive listener engages with the speaker as a lesser participant in the interpersonal communication process. This listener may be attentive, but may also be faking listening to the sender. The inactive listener makes few attempts to give eye contact or clarify any of the sender's statements.

Engaged (38 - 44)

The engaged listener is attentive to the speaker's words and meanings. This person makes an effort to understand the sender's point of view and participates in the interpersonal communication process. The engaged listener practices some direct eye contact and alert posture/stance. They may ask a few clarifying questions and may sometimes respond with clarifying statements.

Active (45 - 50)

The active listener is extremely attentive to others when they are speaking, and focuses on what is being said as well as what is not said (verbal and non-verbal communication). This person expends time and energy participating in the interpersonal communication process, which is usually evidenced by an alert posture/stance, head nodding and a great deal of direct eye contact. They also ask clarifying questions and respond by paraphrasing, restating and reframing.

Active Listening Process

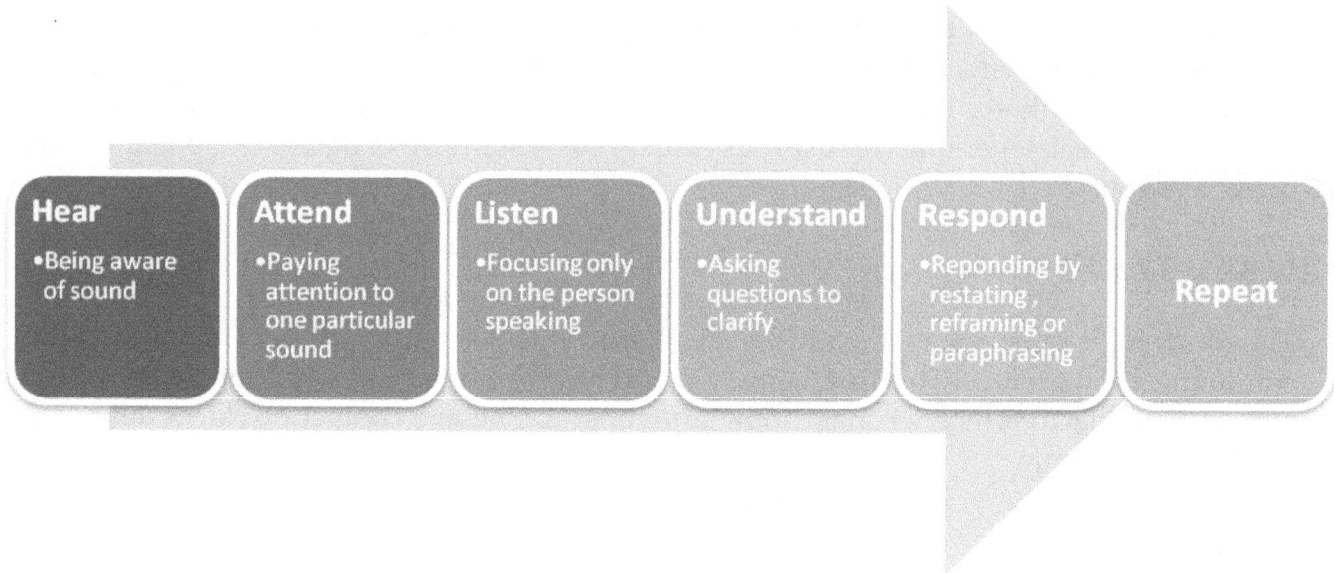

Hear	Attend	Listen	Understand	Respond	Repeat
•Being aware of sound	•Paying attention to one particular sound	•Focusing only on the person speaking	•Asking questions to clarify	•Reponding by restating, reframing or paraphrasing	

Keys to Effective/Productive Active Listening

Be Empathetic

- Make an effort to understand the feelings of others
- Seeing things/issues from others' point of view
- Conveying understanding and acceptance of others

Remove Distractions

- Give the listener your undivided attention
- Turn off television, silence phones, do not allow interruptions by others

Clarify Statements

- Use certain phrases when clarifying what the Sender is saying

    "What I hear you saying is..."
    "It seems like you're feeling..."
    "Tell me if I'm wrong, but are you saying..."
    "Tell me a little bit more about..."

Active Listening Exercise

When listening it is important to focus on the **Who, What, When, Where, Why & How.**

To practice your listening skills, either have someone read the statements listed below to you or read each statement once, and then cover it up and answer the questions.

"I just spoke with my brother in California. He's really upset. He started a new job only three months ago and yesterday he was laid off. He really needed that job."

WHO:
WHAT:
WHEN:
WHERE:
WHY:
HOW:

"I'm worried! My back has been in pain for a week. I don't like going to the doctor and hate hospitals even more. What if I they say I need surgery? The last person I knew that had back surgery died on the operating table. Maybe I'll just bear with the pain."

WHO:
WHAT:
WHEN:
WHERE:
WHY:
HOW:

"I got a call from her today. We had a huge blow up last week and haven't spoken since. I wish I wouldn't have said those horrible things but I was so mad. I hope we can patch things up and move on."

WHO:
WHAT:
WHEN:
WHERE:
WHY:
HOW:

<u>Notes</u>

Be Prepared! –
Stress Management

Learning how to effectively manage stress as it relates to anger is essential to preparing yourself to deal with the pressures of everyday life.

Goals:
Define stress and it's connection to anger
Identify sources of stress
Practice relaxation exercises

Be Prepared! Stress Management

What is Stress?

Stress happens when our body's physical & emotional reaction to circumstances or events frighten, confuse, endanger, or excite and place demands on the body.

> *Stress can be good or bad. It can be caused by a job promotion or a job loss, the birth of a baby or the death of a parent. Stress is about our response to these kinds of events.*

Stress often intensifies our anger reactions. When we are under some degree of stress and encounter an anger inducing situation, our response or reaction to that situation may seem "blown out of proportion".

What causes you stress?

_____

_____

_____

_____

How stressed are you? Take the stress survey.

Holmes and Rahe stress inventory

Instructions: The following scale was developed by Holmes and Rahe to investigate the relationship between events which happen to us, stress and susceptibility to illness. Look over the events listed below. Mark the item if it has happened to you within the **last twelve months**. (You can multiply it by the number of times it has occurred to be accurate!)

Event	Points	Yes/No	Score
1. Death of a spouse	100	____	____
2. Divorce	72	____	____
3. Marital separation	65	____	____
4. Death of a close family member	63	____	____
5. Personal injury or illness	53	____	____
6. Marriage	50	____	____
7. Marital reconciliation	45	____	____
8. Change in health of family member	44	____	____
9. Pregnancy	40	____	____
10. Gain of new family member	39	____	____
11. Job Change	38	____	____
12. Change in financial status	37	____	____
13. Death of a close friend	36	____	____
14. Increase in arguments with significant other	35	____	____
15. Mortgage or loan of major purchase (home, etc.)	31	____	____
16. Foreclosure of mortgage or loan	30	____	____
17. Change in responsibilities of your job	29	____	____
18. Son or daughter leaving home	29	____	____
19. Trouble with in-laws	29	____	____
20. Outstanding personal achievement	28	____	____
21. Spouse begins or stops work outside the home	26	____	____
22. Revision of personal habits	24	____	____
23. Trouble with boss	23	____	____
24. Change in work hours or conditions	20	____	____
25. Change in residence	20	____	____
26. Change in sleeping habits	16	____	____
27. Change in eating habits	15	____	____
28. Vacation	13	____	____
29. Christmas	12	____	____
30. Minor violations of the law	11	____	____
Total			____

Scoring:

0-149 no significant problem
150-199 mild stress 35% chance of illness or health change
200-299 moderate stress 50% chance of illness or health change
300+ major stress 80% chance of illness or health change.

The higher your score on the survey, the harder you should work to stay well!

Holmes, T. & Rahe, R. (1967). "Holmes-Rahe Social Readjustment Rating Scale", Journal of Psychosomatic Research, vol. II.

Do you feel your score was accurate to the stress level you feel? _____

How did you feel during these times of stress?

_____

_____

Sources of Stress

Environmental – Weather, pollens, traffic, noise, pollution

Social – Deadlines, finances, job, demands for time and attention

Physiological – Illness, menopause, aging, lack of exercise, poor nutrition, inadequate sleep

Intrapersonal – Irrational thoughts and beliefs

What source does most of your stress come from? _____

Controlling Stress

How do you currently handle stress?

_____

_____

20 Ways to Control Stress – Pick one that you can use this week

Do only one thing at a time instead of multi-tasking.	Slow down. Talk slowly.
Focus only on the present and what you can do now.	Establish & maintain a daily schedule that is realistic.
Exercise!	Get adequate sleep, rest and nutrition.
Say "No" more often.	Don't try to know all the answers.
Talk less, listen more.	Learn to meet your own needs.
Always have a plan B.	SMILE!
Ask questions.	Simplify, simplify, simplify.
Do nothing that leads you to tell a lie.	Be prepared to wait.
Delegate responsibility.	Do unpleasant tasks early in the day.
Eliminate destructive self-talk.	Allow quiet time for yourself.

Relaxation Exercises

Below are several different kinds of relaxation and deep breathing exercises. Read over them and make a commitment to practice at least one of them this week.

Meditation

Meditation can help calm you and clear your mind of anger.

Steps

1. *Find a quiet place. Wear loose, comfortable clothing. Sit or lie down.*
2. *Close your eyes. Take slow, deep breaths.*
3. *Concentrate on a single word, object or calming thought.*
4. *Don't worry if other thoughts or images enter your mind while you are doing this. Just relax and return to what you were focusing on.*
5. *Continue until you feel relaxed and refreshed.*

Deep-Breathing Exercises

These can help keep your anger from getting out of control.

Steps

1. *Sit comfortably or lie on your back.*
2. *Breathe in slowly and deeply for a count of 7.*
3. *Hold your breath for count of 7.*
4. *Breathe out slowly for a count of 7, pushing out all the air.*
5. *Repeat several times until you feel calm and relaxed.*

Progressive Muscle Relaxation

Progressive Muscle Relaxation involves tensing and relaxing each muscle group, starting at your head and working your way down to your toes.

Steps

1. *Wear loose, comfortable fitting clothing. Sit in a comfortable chair or lie down.*
2. *Tense the muscles in your face for 5 -10 seconds. Then relax them for about 20 seconds.*
3. *Tense the muscles in the back of your neck for 5-10 seconds. Then relax for about 20 seconds. Notice the difference in how your muscles feel when relaxed.*
4. *Move down to your shoulders. Tense and relax the muscles the same way you did in step 3.*
5. *Repeat the same steps with the other muscle groups in your body – in your fingers, hands, arms, chest, stomach, lower back, buttocks, calves, feet and toes – one at a time.*

Visualization

Visualization is a technique that uses your imagination to help you relax and reduce your anger.

Steps

1. *Sit in a comfortable chair or lie down.*
2. *Imagine a pleasant, peaceful scene, such as a lush forest or a sandy beach. Picture yourself in this setting.*
3. *Focus on the scene. Continue until you feel refreshed and relaxed.*

<u>Notes</u>

Be Prepared! – Conflict Transformation

Conflict, like anger, is another one of those inevitable issues that come with being human. As long as we are in relationship with others some conflict will arise. In order to be prepared to handle conflict effectively we must change our perception of it and make an effort to see the other side of the conflict.

Goals: Define conflict & conflict Transformation
           Identify the 5 causes of conflict
           Practice conflict transformation techniques

Be Prepared! Conflict Transformation

WHAT IS CONFLICT?

Conflict is a **competitive or opposing action of incompatibles**.

Viewing the **same thing** from two different viewpoint and those differing viewpoints are slowing or halting the progress of that particular thing.

What Conflict is NOT!

➤ **It is NOT the dislike or disdain for another**. We may clash with one's personality or may not like the actions of another, but that DOES NOT meet the criteria for a conflict.

➤ **It is NOT an argument or dispute.** The dispute or argument may be how the conflict is communicated or manifested, but it is not the actual conflict. For example, a conflict issue may not be communicated in an argument but may be communicated passive aggressively by talking to others about it rather than the person you are in conflict with.

What is the CONFLICT about?

Conflict happens when you have opposing views from another person caused by differences in your goals, resources, ideas, needs, and desires or **THE GRIND**.

GOALS – Outcomes we would like to see happen: to graduate from college, to run a 10k race, to start my own business, to complete a project on time. Example: *By the time I am 40, I would like to be the president of a major Fortune 500 company.*

RESOURCES – A source of help or supply. Example: *time, energy, money, staff, etc.*

IDEAS – Thoughts, opinions, or plans of actions. Example: *I have an idea to change the way we greet customers. Their idea about how the project should work doesn't make sense.*

NEEDS – The minimum requirements of life & health. Water, food, shelter, clothing, medical care, etc. Example: *I need to eat lunch at a specific time each day because of the medication I've been prescribed.*

DESIRES – The longing, wishing, wanting or hoping for a particular thing or circumstance. Example: *I really hope I get this job! The wish for some peace and quiet.*

Looking at the list of Causes of Conflict, which one(s) are most of your conflicts about?

_____

_____

What is Conflict Transformation?

Conflict Transformation is the idea that the differences we have in a conflict can be used to make a situation progress rather than regress. In order to transform a conflict, one person must take the lead to begin the process.

Conflict is a decision NOT to make a decision!

Often, people wait to deal with conflict because the situation has become volatile or overwhelming. You have the opportunity to take the lead and diminish the conflict through transformation.

How is Velcro ® like Conflict Transformation?

Velcro® is a great example of how two things that are opposed to each other actually come together to make something else work perfectly.

Velcro® consists of hooks and loops. The Hooks are on the very hard side with neatly situated rows. The Loops are on the soft, hairy and unkempt looking side. When you look at them and feel them they are totally different to one another. However, the hooks EXIST to engage with the loops, and vice versa. When the hooks and loops come together, they fasten two separate things to make them into one.

> *Our "sameness" helps us reflect but our "differences" help us grow and change.*

Conflict Transformation Exercise

1. *Think back over the last month and identify a conflict that has occurred in your life.*

   _____

   _____

   _____

   _____

   _____

2. *For the conflict you listed in item 1, write out how each of these is related to the incompatibles below: (Remember to be honest! If you are not honest about what your sources of conflict are, your transformation of conflict will be unrealistic!) First list your G.R.I.N.D. and then list what you think the opposing G.R.I.N.D. might be.*

What is Your G.R.I.N.D.?	What is Their G.R.I.N.D.?
Goals –	Goals –
Resources–	Resources–
Ideas–	Ideas –
Needs–	Needs–
Desires –	Desires –

3. Circle the part of *your* G.R.I.N.D. that will move the situation out of conflict.

4. Circle the part of *their* G.R.I.N.D. that will move the situation out of conflict.

5. Be "**US**" focused; think about how combining your G.R.I.N.D. with theirs will move the situation out of conflict and what the result might be.

_____

_____

_____

Notes